Why does ice melt?

Jim Pipe

Copper Beech Books
Brookfield, Connecticut

Why does ice melt?

The children are eating ice pops in the kitchen. But they soon start to melt in the warm room.

"Eat them quickly, or they will drip all over the floor," says Amy.

Why is my ice pop dripping?

1

Let's see how the children find out.

Let's put ice cubes in the blue cups and water in the red cups.

I'll put the other cups in the freezer.

I'll put one cup of ice and one cup of water in the warm room.

2

Look! Both cups on the table are full of water, so ice turns to water when it gets warm.

Both cups in the freezer have ice in them, so water turns to ice when it gets very cold.

Why it works

Water turns to solid ice when it gets very cold. When ice gets warm, it turns to water. We say it becomes liquid. Most things melt when they get hot—think of butter, chocolate, and candle wax. Even rocks melt when they get hot enough. Think of lava in a volcano.

Solve the puzzle!

What makes things melt quicker? To find out, put a lump of chocolate
• on a cold plate
• in your hand.
What happens? Turn to page 22 for the answer.

What happens when water freezes?

Outside, it is very cold. The pond in the park has frozen. Steve's mom says, "Be very careful, don't go near the edge." The children can see fish swimming under the ice.

Why is the ice only on the top of the water?

3

Now it's solid ice, and it has pushed up over the top!

The ice must take up more space than the water did.

Water turns to solid ice when it freezes. But it also spreads out and takes up more room. This makes ice lighter than water for its size, so it floats. Because water takes up more room when it freezes, it can burst pipes in very cold weather.

Solve the puzzle!

Why are icebergs such a danger to ships? Put a lump of ice in a glass of water and see how much of it floats below the water. Does this give you a clue?

Can you stop ice from melting?

The next day, it snows. At the park, the children build a snowman. They roll the snow into big, icy balls. Their snowman looks great!

How can we stop our snowman from melting?

11

My big lump has hardly melted, so wrapping it up kept it frozen.

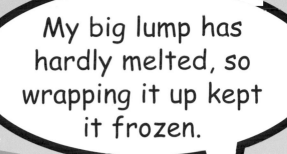

2

My cubes have melted more than Amy's big lump, so small lumps must melt faster, too.

Why it works

Wrapping plastic around the ice keeps the warm air from reaching it, so it melts slower. If the children wrap a coat around the snowman, it will melt slower, too. Also, the bigger a lump of ice is, the slower it melts. So a big snowman melts slower than a small one does.

Solve the puzzle!

Why do people put salt on icy roads? Put two ice cubes into separate glasses. Pour lots of salt on one of the cubes and see which cube melts faster.

15

Where did the snowman go?

When the children go back to the park, the sun is out. The snow has all gone, and the snowman has vanished.

Where did our snowman go?

It melted. The water must have trickled away.

15

the children find out.
Let's put an ice cube in the sun. On a saucer it can't trickle away or get soaked up.
Now the ice is a little pool of water.
I'll mark around it with a crayon.

Why it works

Heat from the sun turns the ice cube into water, then dries up the water. When water dries up, it turns into a gas called water vapor.

We say it evaporates. This water is in the air even though we can't see it. Melting snow turns to water, too. Some of it soaks into the ground, but most of it turns to water vapor.

Solve the puzzle!

What makes water evaporate faster? Get two saucers and put a few drops of water on each. Put one saucer in the sun and the other in the shade. Which drops vanish first?

Why do windows steam up?

The children go indoors to play. It is much warmer inside. "Look, the window has steamed up," says Jo. Steve draws a big face on the glass.

Why are drops of water on the inside of the window?

Maybe the water came through the glass.

the children find out.
1
The ice cubes in these glasses will make them cold. I'll put a lid on one so the water can't get out.
2
I'll pour warm water into this glass to make it warm.
Let's see what happens if we wait a few minutes.

The warm glass isn't wet. So the glass needs to be cold for the drops to appear.

The cold glasses are wet on the outside, even the one with a lid. The water must come from air outside the glass.

Why it works

The air is full of water vapor that we can't easily see. When warm air touches a cold surface such as glass, this water vapor turns into water drops. We call this condensation. The water on the window comes from warm air inside the house. It turned into water when it met the cold window.

Solve the puzzle!

Why are chips put in sealed bags? Take some out of the bag and leave them on a plate overnight. What happens?

Did you solve the puzzles?

What makes things melt faster?

The hotter things are, the faster they melt. So chocolate melts faster on a warm hand than it does on a cold plate. It is the warm air in the kitchen that makes the ice pops on page 5 melt quickly.

Why are icebergs such a danger to ships?

You know that ice floats on water from page 8. Looking at an ice cube, you will also see that most of the ice floats under the surface. So if a ship hits an iceberg, the hard ice can make a big hole in the ship under the water.

Why do people put salt on icy roads?

An ice cube melts faster when you put salt on it. Cars can skid on ice, so people put salt on the roads to melt the ice quickly and make the roads safe. Do you remember what made the ice melt slower on page 13?

What makes water evaporate faster?

The hotter water is, the faster it evaporates. So water in the sun dries up faster than water in the shade.

When water gets very hot, it boils and evaporates very quickly.

Why are chips put in bags?

On page 21, water vapor in the air turned into drops of water. If you take chips out of their bag, they soak up this water vapor and turn soggy.

23

Index

© Aladdin Books Ltd 2002

10 9 8 7 6 5 4 3 2 1

Designed and produced by
Aladdin Books Ltd
28 Percy Street
London W1T 2BZ

First published in
the United States in 2002 by
Copper Beech Books,
an imprint of
The Millbrook Press
2 Old New Milford Road
Brookfield, Connecticut 06804

ISBN 0-7613-2723-1 (Library bdg.)
ISBN 0-7613-1836-4 (Paper ed.)

Cataloging-in-Publication data is
on file at the Library of Congress.

Printed in U.A.E.
All rights reserved

Literacy Consultant
Jackie Holderness
Westminster Institute of Education,
Oxford Brookes University, England

Science Consultant
Michael Brown

Science Testers
Ben, Toby, and Elliott Fussell

Design
Flick, Book Design and Graphics

Illustration
Jo Moore